Young Voices of Human Conflict

A collection of poems by Christel House Academy South Middle School Students

Created and edited by the 7th and 8th grade students at
Christel House Academy South
Indianapolis, Indiana
2014

Student Editors

Khairat Raji, Teagan Mitchener, Kiah Davis, Malik McClain,
Sara Klinge, Shania Burton, Emily Amaya, Rachael Bruce,
Taylor Cruz, Danielle Schmaelzle, and Folu Famoye

© 2014 by Christel House Academy
All rights reserved.

Published in the United States by
Christel House Academy South
2717 S. East St.
Indianapolis, IN 46225
www.chacademy.org

ISBN 978-0-692-20333-0

Special Thanks

Sharing the Dream Grant Program
National Association of Elementary School Principals
MetLife Foundation

Christel House International

Arts for Learning
Beth El-Zedeck Temple
Islamic Society of North America

Table of Contents

INTRODUCTION: A WORD FROM "THE TEACHERS" 7
PREFACE 9

Poetry

TAKE ME TO THE RUINS 11
THE UNKNOWN INSIDE 13
ISRAELI. PALESTINIAN. 14
MAKING PEACE 16
TICK TOCK 17
A DREAM 19
MY PALESTINIAN AND ISRAELI TEARS 21
WHAT WOULD HAPPEN IF? 24
AIR 25
UNTITLED 27
FROM BEAUTIFUL PALESTINE 28
(PEACE IS HARD TO FIND) 30
1954 31
WHY THE WAR? 32
STONE 34
UNTITLED 37
I REMEMBER… 39
UNTITLED 41
TWO SHADES OF RED 43
HOPE 45
STARTING PEACE 46
THE DAWN OF A NEW DAY 48

NO MORE WAR	49
PEACE TO BE FOUND	50
FROM FIGHTING TO FRIENDS	51
OUR HOME	53
THE LEGEND	55
UNTITLED	56
DREAMING OUT LOUD	57
PEACE IS ALL WE NEED	59
SIX ISRAELI GIRLS	60
TRYING TO REMEMBER TO GO A DIFFERENT WAY	61
UNTITLED	62
COLOR PALLET	64
ISRAELI AND PALESTINIAN POEM	65
70	66
STRUGGLE	68
WHY DO WE LIVE?	69
WE WANT PEACE	70
FORGETTING	72
LIVE FOR THE FUTURE?	74
CONFUSION	75
FINDING YOUR PEACE	76
PEACE IS LIKE A GOLDEN BAR	77
UNTITLED	79
PEACE MY LAND AND YOURS	81

INTRODUCTION: A WORD FROM "THE TEACHERS"

Anytime teachers deal with current events in a classroom, students' engagement, curiosity, and interest are peaked. They respond to the visceral and substantive nature of issues from recent history and the modern day which they can witness with their own eyes in a profound and thought provoking way. The Palestinian-Israeli conflict is one such subject matter. However, to teach such content in the classroom requires an understanding of the complexities that surround it, and a particular sensitivity to the nature of the conflict. We undertook this project with such cautions in mind, fully aware of the obstacles that lay before us. Our students responded with maturity, inquisitiveness, and a sincere desire to learn. Of course, we would like students to develop comprehensive knowledge of the historical information surrounding this conflict, as well as poetic elements. After all, we embarked on this project with the intent to teach our respective contents in a unique and engaging way. But academics and standards aside, we would like students to come away from this exploration with a heightened sense of the complexity surrounding much of human life. This issue is sensitive, thought-provoking, emotional, and complicated. It is not something that can be explained in black and white terms. Approaching this subject with that outlook in mind, and forcing students to think critically, challenge assumptions, and examine issues with scrutiny, are skills that will serve them well not only in their academic lives, but our students' personal lives as well.

Even with these distinguished goals, our students are still kids. They are forming and building knowledge, creating a system of understanding through which they can piece together information from the world surrounding them. We decided that students would benefit from an artistic medium through which to express their growing knowledge. For this reason, students created poems from the perspective of Palestinians and Israelis who have been affected by the conflict. We are very proud of our students' poetry, and hope that all readers of this text approach it with diligence and the understanding that 7th and 8th grade students, previously unfamiliar with this information, worked hard to write them with empathy and compassion towards the real humans affected on both sides of this real conflict.

- The Middle School Teachers of Christel House Academy South

PREFACE

This book is full of inspiring poems by concerned children who are promoting peace, and who also want to inform you about the Israeli-Palestinian conflict. The children of the Middle School at Christel House Academy South in the United States want to raise awareness about the violence in the conflict, and help all of the people who have been affected. We hope this book will inspire our readers to know what people are going through, and see that even though there is conflict going on, there is still hope. This conflict has affected many children and adults' lives and we hope to make that impact less and less.

We, the students, studied this topic for two months and have put a lot of thought and concern into these poems. We hope to accomplish many things with our inspirational words. We young writers hope that you not just read these poems, but also share them with others so that they can hear our message too.

The middle school at Christel House Academy South hopes to help all of people and children involved in the Israeli-Palestinian conflict. We want to change those peoples' lives so that they can live in a better, safer environment. We want to end their sorrow and change their lives through our motivating and uplifting poetry.

-Christel House Academy South Middle School Students

TAKE ME TO THE RUINS
Teagan Mitchener

As I walked through what is left of Shanti
I could hear the debris cry,
The *wailing,*
s
c
r
e
a
m
s
and all the *goodbyes.*
It all came in a flash.
How did she go so fast?
Without a goodbye, just-gone.
I felt as if the wind was
p
u
s
h
i
n
g
me to my knees.
I sit there and cry
Wondering

If she would have said goodbye.
If she would be here today.
If it all went away.

I pick myself up
And as I walk away
I get this… feeling.
I can't exactly tell you how it felt.

It was *warm*.
I believe it was *Hope*.
In this conflict there is still *hope*.
Do you have *hope*?
Today as I walk away I say goodbye.
I will **<u>never</u>** return to Shanti, the ruins.
<u>Never</u> say, "Take me to the ruins".
Because *Hope* has taken over and
this
is
just
the
beginning.

THE UNKNOWN INSIDE
Danielle Schmaelzle

STOP THIS.
This is painful.
You hurt me.
My people. Your people. Injured. Dead. In pain. And losing.
Tearing Apart Families & Relationships. We know who you are...

The face of pain you bring, is
UNKNOWN.
Where this came from.
UNKNOWN.
HOW you could do this.
UNKNOWN.

The death you bring and
about the pain we sing.

HOPING!
SOMEDAY
neither of our people would have to lose...

So we wouldn't have to run and hide.
So we wouldn't have to aim for where it really
hurts. AIMING. For
CHILDREN and all must fall.

ISRAELI. PALESTINIAN.

What is the difference?
  Just words.
  Just people.

            Going through the same...
RIGHTS. LIVES.
  GONE.

No Regret. You Don't Care.
  Inhumane. Crazy.
                Just a few things...
            H
            O
            L
            O
            C
            A
            U
            S
            T
                            - 6,000,000
        Suicide
            B
            B
            O
            M

B
I
N
G
S

- Too many

Stop this. UNBLIND us. Set us

F
R
E
E

Our lives… a T-I-C-K-I-N-G bomb.
You defused it. You gave your life to us.
Give us HOPE. Let us live peacefully on our land.

How we were supposed to.

With HOPE. Now we have...

HOPE -
Finally. Maybe.

MAKING PEACE
Jesus Nunez

As I see people running,

it reminds me about the Six Day War,

and all the missiles going to the children...

I see people injured or maybe dead.

Some Palestinian family is trying to make peace

but I think about it, and

I'm not the only one getting bombed.

it was the Israelis getting bombed too - are we all that different?

There was a man who lost his wife by a Palestinian suicide bomber,

but instead of getting revenge, he made peace with the Palestinian suicide bomber's family.

The only thing to stop the conflict is to stop fighting

and start to make

                    PEACE.

TICK TOCK
Jalen Mitchell

Sitting in my room.

All I can hear is the ticking of the clock. (Tick Tock)

I can still hear Dad trying to break out where the sand is guarding the door. (Tick Tock)

Is it day?

Is it night?

I don't know. (Tick Tock)

Not enough food for the family.

So I don't eat. (Tick Tock)

I can hear my sister crying because she wants dad to stop. (Tick Tock)

All I want is peace.

                Standing at the bus stop in Jerusalem.

            Fearing that there is going to be a bomb on the bus. (Tick Tock)

                    Scared like a child in the dark.

                          The bus pulls up.

        Don't know to get in or don't know to stay out. (Tick Tock)

                                I get in.

                I'm starring at everyone. (Tick Tock)

                  I make it to my destination.

                      All I want is peace.

All we want is peace.
Peace is like a golden ball, like the sun.
Always out of reach.

A DREAM
Folu Famoye

I can tell that
outside of my window, into a gloomy evening
across a small hill
there is a house,
an *Arab* house
it looks clean but I know that its stained
stained with the colors of fear and hate
I see
a girl
crying
blue and gray she's like me
but <u>not</u> like me, it's in her blood, not
a hard rough blanket of sadness covers her heart
her heart must be filled with hate
or perhaps...
a desire for peace?
                                      a dream of hope and happiness
                         a desperate cry for peace turns my head to the west
                                      so I can illustrate thoughts
                                          but instead I see them
                                              the men, the *Israelites*
                                          watching and fighting back
                                  I want to run but there is no use
                                              it may be like this

forever
but we can change
the innocent souls don't pass on
like they should
and they won't until they see that we
have changed
until they see
peace
We are all humans we all bleed red
we are all from *Abraham*
we all share a similar dream

"If we who have paid the greatest price can talk to each other
why can't anyone else?"
let's share this dream
for peace.

MY PALESTINIAN AND ISRAELI TEARS
Emily Amaya

I'm but a mere blur of blue and swirling dust
As the Israeli soldiers past me, towards
STORMED
Their tanks and guns.   These are
My people – I feel
overwhelmed.
My brother has just joined these men,
And now the war leaves him in the
dirt,
Like a lost dove in   wonderland –   Wondering where to go.
What do I DO? What, watch him do the careless?
    Do as other soldiers   do?
Of this land, killed in vain.
Enduring the lame pain.

A
    loose tear leaks from eye –

A reminder
of who I've been, what I have

To become.

My
heartbreak in a simple form,

Like a fire,
as a beast, this rage swirls within.

I had a SISTER.

     Laiba...

          THEY killed
  her. With a bomb

           And
    injustice.

      We fight over this feud, but
    we do not

          SEE the
harm done to us. I will fight   Until

          DEATH.

    I FEAR THEM, THE others.
     The Palestinians…

      The Israelites.

    I AM an Israeli-Palestinian. I am here, and are not both sides at fault?

      We blame and blame,

     But do not   act.

   I cry over our Six-Day War, over the

      BOMBS, on innocent children.

 Not only do I cry, the fruitless, yet fruitful tears
       of Israel

      – stand my friend.

     Aye, kin.

AND friend Palestinian.

Aye, my brother.

More than 60 years.
A sweet sound rings in my ears

I cry Palestinian and Israeli Tears.

WHAT WOULD HAPPEN IF?
Brooklyn Davis

The people will fight
But not for death
For peace

Dead bodies lifted in the air wrapped in flags
As if they were on a flagpole flowing in the wind
The death of....
Causes us to think, "What would happen if?"

They can only go so far
They don't ever stop

There's plenty of blame
And nothing will be the same
So many people dead, hurt, emotionally drained

Protesters and martyrs care
No one can bare
People stare at their blood stained carpets
They think, "What would happen if?"

AIR
Ana Gomez

You know who I am.
I surround everything and everyone
for you survive because of me.
I am able to flow freely
riding clouds through the sky
like a rider rides a horse through the plains.

But day by day, I am saddened
and angered by the war for land.
<u>BOOM!</u> Goes an explosion
as it harms all near it.
I carry the fumes of smoke,
I carry the cries and screams of
anger, revenge, grievance, agony, and sorrow.

Dust swirls with my winds
dirtying my sweet Air,
my raging winds help not.
I watch many thrive to survive
another day of war.

I carry the ashes of the lost,
watch helplessly as children are killed.
For my winds can do nothing
to stop the bullets from piercing them.

For I, Air, am useless to stop these
devices that kill innocence.

But even though I can't
stop these deaths and killings,
I carry the shouts of the people
who want to give peace,
hope, forgiveness and unity.

I watch as these people,
of both groups, join together
sharing the feeling of sorrow and anger
but replacing it with hope and peace.
They help each other, tell others of the peace
that may be or could be.

UNTITLED

Ashley Guevara Stone

People are dying
Please let us stop the fighting
With all the hatred and crying
No one sees how much we're trying

Why have war?
It's all happened before
Why feel sad for your losses
When others have losses too

Like a carousel going around
Will the world ever come as one?

FROM BEAUTIFUL PALESTINE
Alan Hodge

Blue clear skies not a cloud in sight
people walking all around some of them
going to the market, some going to the mosque
children laughing and playing all around

People are scared of suicide bombers because
they never know where or when it can happen
they are scared of the next bombing

Going to the city of Jerusalem to meet with an Israeli
to see how they feel as victims and how we feel about it
let's see how they feel

There is one person that
seems scared... I ask him about it, he says that he's scared of...
In the beautiful city of Jerusalem people are walking all around
people driving some taking the bus, they're losing.
I say, "Losing what or who?". He says, "Loved ones or even
myself".

We never know when they're going to attack we don't want it
I wish we could have peace I WANT NO MORE DEATH
No human should have to put up with what both of us do

We don't want war anymore

NO MORE DEATH

(PEACE IS HARD TO FIND)
Alima Jones

Everyone's goal is peace like an olive branch out of (Reach)
  Without an agreement by all, solutions seem impossible
   Palestinians continue to fight the Israelis for (Independence)

Israelis continue to respond in (Defense)
   Bombings in Israel................
  Lead to more (invasions) in Palestinian towns
  Everyone wants (Control) of their Holy Land............................
   But haven't found a way to talk about it without (Conflict)
  Peace is like (True Friends) you want it but can't always have it
       Everyone's goal is peace

1954

Anahi Murillo

my mother's eyes dancing with fear
the rain drops on my brother's face
the frightened face of my sister

(WHY)

why attack my Jewish village outside of
TEL-AVIV

I'm Thinking

I still have to promote peace
I want change
I want to leave my footprint in this world
I want to be known as the little Jewish girl who made peace with the Palestinian people
I want a key to this puzzle

crouching, hands on my head
nails penetrating my scalp...

1954

WHY THE WAR?
Christian Cox

I can hear a whisper from the breeze.
I can remember the memories of my people being forced on their knees.
A conflict begins at the dawn of day.
I wonder if this battle will ever go away.

I don't understand the anger we build to go there.
Do people understand the personalities and faiths we share?
We both share the religion of Abraham.
What is the point trying to get children to fight as if each is a man?
We both want the same lands.
Why don't we just make up and shake hands?

Why don't we just come to a halt?
Instead of bringing children in it with anger and assault.
What happened to our people once before?
Let's just be friends and get along. I ask nothing more.
So let us give it a try
Because we both don't want to see our people die.

I can hear a whisper from the breeze.
I can remember the memories of my people being forced on their knees.
A conflict begins at the dawn of day.

I wonder if this battle will ever go away.

Why the war?

STONE
Collin Lierman

My journey
is long
and hard.

A week ago
I was part of something big
I was just as important
as anyone else.

This all changed
one fine day.
I was going about my business
and then it happened.

Eeeee-BOOM
The rocket hit right by me.
The explosion flung me from my crumbling home,
far from where I was.

My journey
is long
and hard.

The next time I moved
It was a bulldozer

pushing me
with the rest of the rubble.

Because I survived.
The ones I am now with
Survived.
I was among those chosen to survive.
I can't die, but I would be in no better position wishing I was.

I survived.
Many, however
were not so lucky.
They can't die, but they wish they could.
There should be no other being,
person or rock,
that should ever have to experience
what happened that day.
      Because I am a stone,
Blown off of a building.

This fighting I heard about
When I was part of that building
It should stop.

No being
Palestinian or Israeli
Rock or person
should have to go through that
What I went through

What the people went through
All of us
It shouldn't be happening

We're all the same
Rocks don't kill rocks
Why should people kill people?
This thing they want
Peace
It needs to happen.

Now.

Not later.

Now.

My journey
is long
and hard.

UNTITLED
Danielle Williamson

As I walk around the streets of Palestine,
I see the faces of small children and their parents.
Filled with fear.
Hope.
No Defeat.
"I will not be defeated."

"Never to be shot down"
"Always on my feet"

That is what I read from them.
That is what I hear them calling out.
For HOPE.
For FORGIVENESS.
For PEACE.
I cry Palestinian tears.

And the same for me.
I walk around and see my people
shot down by the "Enemy".
WHY?.
To me, that is an entire new world.
I have been taught to HATE.
Nothing more.
All I want is love.

"I don't understand this fight"

"Why the war?"

"What are we becoming?"

"I will not give in."
I cry Israeli tears.

We all have grown to HATE.
Even people we don't know.
WHY?
What has this conflict brought to us?
We need to stick together and
WIN the fight.
I want to help them.

We need to overcome FEAR.
Overcome DEFEAT.
Come together, and make peace.
Stop the deaths.
I want to understand the other side.

Together, we cry each other's tears.

I REMEMBER...
Elycia Simmons

I Remember
I Remember That Day
Nightmares They Haunt Me
Some Even More Scary
In a Kinda Weird Way

I Remember That Day
The Day
The Day Those Scary Bulldozers
They Rolled in

We Just Stood There
Rachel And I
And Watched Debris
Fall In The Sky

Out of Nowhere
Courage Smacked Her
She Stepped Up

While We Yelled
Rachel, Rachel
She Professed
Right In Front Of It

It
The Bulldozer

It
Ran Over
Rachel, My Friend

My Land
Rained Debris everywhere

Rachel Dead
I Couldn't Believe
I Should've Stepped up
Protested with Her
Died with Her

But Now It's My Time
To Live For Her

UNTITLED
Hershella Griffin

Waiting to be caught
Why Can't We Feel Safe?

My house has been bombed
I feel sad as if I was gone
My parents are lying there
This is not fair

War starts soon   We've been
                         bombed
                                                             Children and
              parents are dying
Why can't I feel safe?   Why can't
                    we feel safe?

I can't walk outside
It's too dangerous
My heart is fading away
Blood is everywhere

I am all alone   The bus
                         exploded
                                                             People have
                       been hurt
Why can't I feel safe?   Why can't
                    we feel safe?

The war has started
I hear yelling and screaming

I hide in a corner waiting

While the rest was being fought   Fathers and
           Mothers are upset

                                              Throwing
           things and crying

Why can't I feel safe?   Why can't
           we feel safe?

         The Israelis are everywhere
          My body feels weak
           Everyone is dying
         While I'm still here crying

I don't know what to do   We don't
           know what to do

We Palestinians are lost   We
           Israelis are lost

Why can't we feel safe?   Why can't
   we feel safe?

                                     We shall fight for
              peace
       because we once loved the deceased
    The children, fathers, and sons that are already gone
     This may continue like a never ending song

TWO SHADES OF RED
Taylor Cruz

I stand on the corner
of my street and see a girl my age.
I wave, she waves at me, we both smiled.
Her smile is like the sun shine.

I am about to go over there
but I feel a hand grab onto mine.
So I turn around and see my mom.
She tells me with eyes afraid,
"She is a Palestinian".
Her mom stops her too.
I look at her, she looks at me.
We both walk away.
It's so very dark,
like we are separated
by our skin color.
But in this situation, it's our religion

Why can't I play with her?
What did she do?
I see the bombs and the shootings
but is it her who tells those men
to shoot at people,
or send the bombs?

Are her people being attacked
by the shooters and the bombers too?
Why does this happen to us?
Maybe her family is not bad like those
people who kill.

Maybe mom shouldn't judge
her because she is Palestinian.

Maybe we are not so different after all.
We are two shades of red,
But not the same.

HOPE

Jeremy Hilliard

Israeli –
Palestinian –
doesn't matter

we don't judge you by your religion
we don't judge you by the way you look
we don't judge you by the color of your skin

both sons of Abraham
stop all this fighting
it doesn't solve anything
fighting makes things worse

Everyone must have hope
hope for the future
hope for happiness
hope for safety

Mothers hope for children
Children hope for candy
Husbands hope for wives
Wives hope for husbands

Boom, more people die!

STARTING PEACE
Jeff Davis

Bombs fall from the sky
tens of thousands on the ground
and their relatives lay around
while we run through the town

all the buildings hit the ground
as we watch Israelis attack our men
and they kill them, ten by ten
BOOM!
we're here as our people shake in fear

it feels like the end is finally here
as bombs fall like snow
sooner or later it has to go
as I think in my mind

why do we fight over this land
it does not matter
it will soon just be sand
so come on Israel
come and grab our hand

and if we fight over this land
that will soon just be sand
it will be like an hour glass

each breath can be are last

I wonder if they feel our pain
all we do is fight
we are like a lost kite without a string
cut loose and out of proportion

we try to make peace
but it chokes us with revenge
like a snake and it prays
that sooner or later we give up

and the violence starts all over
I stop and think they are just like us
we all fight and we fuss
but I think most all of this violence

come out of falling opinions
we should just stop and think
we are Israelites and they are Palestinians
can we all just stay in Jerusalem

where the Israelis and Palestinians
can live as one and gather up peace like fruit
and let the peace
begin

THE DAWN OF A NEW DAY
Jerome Hilliard

The explosion was too bad to imagine.

I wish it wasn't real, but it was too real.
There are no bad people, only bad decisions.

As I walk through the crimes and tyranny
I try to guide but I am just a spirit in a land that has no right or wrong.

We are just pawns in a bigger game trying to be king.
I'm just an Israeli man in a war I have no part in.

My name is…
Abraham.

NO MORE WAR
Jerae Scott

On bus number 150,
I see a man with a look of suspicion on his face.
I get off and he's still on
I hear a BOOM and I turn around I see the bus is torn to pieces.
All the Israel shop windows are shattered.

People are screaming in Hebrew.
It was a Palestinian suicide bomber.
I yelled.
Nobody came, everyone ran away.
Screams piercing the air like a needle piercing a balloon

Everything is shattered
The streets are covered in a dark red
There's blood on the ground
I see people gathering around crying

why no peace
we want it
the rest of the world wants us to have peace
but they don't; They want war
NO MORE WAR

PEACE TO BE FOUND
Kiah Davis

Why don't they call it war
if they called it war then it would be over
I sit and ponder at the thought, but it never shows

the possibility that they think about the peace between the two people
and that it will make a difference
I wonder about the peace
how its slowly slipping of the cliff of sanity
the fact that it will like be a never ending pit

the peace and coexistence of the lands
can still be possible

the ISRAELIS say the land
is theirs because of their holy text,
and the PALESTINIANS say it's theirs
because they took it when the others left.
I wonder if they will ever agree on who the land belongs to
and I wonder they will be gone before they can
this conflict is as pointless as
a high school fight
a petty fight that is only causing heartache
in the end of all chaos there will be peace
to be found

FROM FIGHTING TO FRIENDS
Kendra Johnson

We live in a place where within a second a normal day could turn into a tragedy
A place where people live in constant fear
A place where one side goes against the other, like a predator after prey
A place where war has been going on for many years.

We think fighting is the key to help this be resolved
but honestly, just think, is land really worth it all?

We keep this battle going
Attacking one another because
Both of us are too stubborn to apologize to each other

Is this conflict keeping you from making friends?
Wouldn't it be nice to shake hands with a Palestinian man?
Or make plans with an Israeli mother while your children play peacefully together?

We live in a place where within a second a normal day could turn into a tragedy
A place where people live in constant fear
A place where one side goes against the other, like a predator after prey
A place where war has been going on for many years

We live
   in a place
      that needs
         peace.

OUR HOME
Khairat Raji

        Clack, Clickity, Clack

      Along the hard and dusty road

My horse's footsteps as he clomps behind me...

            As the bright burning sun beats down on us,

        On my way back...

           Home.

A NEW home in my holy land

                    My promised land...

        Clack, Clickity, Clack

Where I can be free of Hamas

                    Free of the Tyrant

        Free!

The wars will end

                              The arguments will stop

            And we will- **We Will** - be on a path to peace

                        Like the one beneath my feet

The one I share with Israel

                                    The one I share with Palestine

In my home

                                                In my home

                    In our home

                        Jerusalem

THE LEGEND
Laura Davis

I'm a child, a happy child. I enjoy my life. But when I look around. I see everyone praying. I wonder what's wrong, what happened. Why can't we all just get along? The fighting and killing and bombing, it's not necessary. Why can't we all be happy? We laugh, we play, but most of all we pray. Pray and hope to see that one day we all get along and love each other as God loves us! We do not need to fight or kill or chase. We need to love, and share, and help one another keep each other's dignity high. We, the Israelis, think we are better as the captain of football team thinks he is best, but truth is we are no better than the rest.

We all make mistakes and we all have fears. We should get together and let each other hear our sweet cry for help and for peace. We try and we care just as much as everyone else! Just give us the time of day. We are all equal. We are all one race. We all belong to the king. We are siblings and we all want peace!

But you're one side and we are another. But one day, I hope we can all COMBINE as one real and true, because we all have faith. It's a love real and true. We love you and you love us. We can share. What's the fuss? Let's go. Let's conquer our fear to be wrong.

We can all win together. It's a love real and true!!

UNTITLED

Charles Lamont Jackson

put our hands together
and we can take a breath
or can We take a breath
don't pull your hands away
bring them Together
we can
stop the bombings
stop the killing
stand together not
apart

put our hands Together
stop shooting and
start helping
we can share this land
put our hands Together
it would be so grand if
we could just all get
along

acting like Palestinians are the prey
and Israelis the predator
let's make it better
put our hands Together
and just stop.....

DREAMING OUT LOUD
Leah McCallister

Families crying. Weeping. Mourning over hurt and deceased loved ones.
All you can feel is your body shaking as you're in shock and begin to run.
Hoping. Praying. That it is all just a dream.
Finally. It's all over. They walk slowly through the broken streets. Looking at broken homes. And broken hearts. Dozens of families. Huddled together.
Eyes slammed shut. With tear after tear. Through the cracks.
Squeezing as tightly as they can. Saying they will never let go.
Teeth clenched while crying. Trying to catch their breath from running and crying.
Forever. They hold them up for everyone to see.
As soon as you see the shell of what used to be.
Hoping. Praying. That is all just a dream.

I stop observing the horror.
I begin to notice the good.
I wonder what I can do to help.
I notice all the little details that were preserved.
I watch people crying with joy that their friends and family are okay.
I think about the good that can come from this.
I help a woman and her family lift a wall off of their house.
I tell them it will be okay. And remind them that it's not all bad.

I tell a little girl it's not our fault. And it's not the Israelis fault.
I remember in order to rise, you must fall,
if there was no bad, we would feel no good,
what goes up, must come down,
and in order to feel happy, you must frown.

PEACE IS ALL WE NEED
Miguel Anderson

Peace, peace is all we need
peace is all we weep
forgive for all the wrongs
Help the children and the pets like the dogs
Israelis, Palestinians, what's the difference
we are all human, this conflict is nonsense

How are we supposed to live if all we do is fight
This conflict is like a CD player on replay day and night
Have we tried making peace, or is the idea a classified file
This conflict is not new, it has been going for a while
Israelis and Palestinians have all suffered,
they just need to come together, like a bird and its feather

I would do something but I'm just a teenage boy
But you, if you have the power, and want to change
Then do it, no one's stopping you, make a change
I'm tired of seeing fighting, and I think you are too
One can change everything, but what I'm trying to say is
PEACE. Peace is all we need.

SIX ISRAELI GIRLS
Max Montgomery

March 14, 1997
Children
pure and innocent
Massacred by a soldier of Jordan
No one deserves this
This shouldn't happen

The bullets flew in the steel sharp air
Making pools of crimson flood the ground

Peace is all that is needed
Not violence
Violence only
makes
more
Violence

Peace is what we should look for
Peace could be found
In all the
Darkness
Is light

Peace is
the only answer.

TRYING TO REMEMBER TO GO A DIFFERENT WAY
Noah Sizemore

All these burning buildings coming down in the end.
Save yourself, it's the Armageddon again.
It seems to me we're all to blame.
Who's to judge whose hearts at stake?
I see the world burn along with all my memories.
I have no love, why can't I sleep? During this conflict
We want to fight back, so now's the time to act.

UNTITLED
Maya Bingham

This is my land, we have our rights
is what I keep hearing
Guns, violence and bombings all through the night

I'm sleeping in my own nightmare
and can't wake up
if I told someone they'd tell me you're young and confused
so starting today I'm tired of being misused

I'm standing up for myself and I'm standing up now
I want to make peace
I want love, joy, and happiness in the world, somehow

Somewhere out there
I hear my people cry
Why, oh why do they have to die

My country is under attack

Remember what you lost,
Let go of what you can't change,
Take the good with the bad,
It's okay to be sad.

Children with lives go on everyday

We have never spent
A day at home
They're all alone
We always fear
The intifada here
I'm not sure if I can bend
I want the hate all to end

What's another life-time, like mine?
We all die a little sometimes, it's all right.
The hate in hearts
The day is dark
The children
Are pure

COLOR PALLET
Alma Torres

We're Like Two Shades Of Red, Similar But Still
Different
We Both Came From Abraham,
We're Two Different Leaves On The Same Stem
We Need Peace, Hold Hand In Hand,
No More Fighting

ISRAELI AND PALESTINIAN POEM
Audrey Childers

What I have seen in the videos is shrewd

Because of the Palestinians' feud

I saw a lot of children get killed

Even in the schools, they have bombing drills

Jerusalem gets hit with rocks

It's the one thing that's worse than the chicken pox

And

If this could come to an end

The terrible weather with its powerful wind

Would blow this all way

We could see a bright and sunny day

70

Allan Hernandez

70 years of <u>Outrage</u>

70 years of <u>Conflict</u>

As <u>Palestine</u> gets their land chewed up daily

And as <u>Israel</u> mainly faces

<u>Anti-Semitism</u>

Both have horrible <u>Tragedies</u>

Neither side can see the <u>Horrific</u> mind changing war that

Has been

Occurring

Both sides can find the path of <u>Love</u>

Both sides can find the path of <u>Peace</u>

But they think too much

And feel too little

Too many had taken their <u>Lives</u>

Too many had faced <u>Exile</u>

More than land they need <u>Kindness</u>

And <u>Gentleness</u>

Without these Qualities <u>Life</u>

Would be violent and <u>Lost</u>.

Palestinians and Israelis would now learn that

70 years of <u>Outrage</u>

70 years of <u>Massacre</u>

as we know must now come to an <u>End</u>

and as we know

for every <u>Israeli</u> life taken

a new branch will grow

for every <u>Palestinian</u> life taken

a new child will be born

STRUGGLE
Christian Smith

As victims of the conflict
we share fears, we share hopes,
we share dreams.

Though we are not in the same house,
we share the same experiences.

Although we call these experiences by
different names, and look at them through
different eyes, we share the same struggle, you and I.

We share the same lust for peace, but
we are two separate beings.
How can this be?

As victims of the conflict,
we share the same voice, but
what we to do with that voice
is completely up to you.
I am an Israel and you are Palestinian,
but we aren't so different, you and I.

WHY DO WE LIVE?

Rachael Bruce

Why do we live or question our existence?

Why do people live in fear, why should they be afraid to live?
Surviving is not the same as living.

What's the reason for fighting, or killing each other?
What's the point of hurting innocent people over your religion, or land?

Once you shed someone's blood on this land, it's no longer holy or sacred.

WE WANT PEACE
Rosamaria Jackman

My eyes are full of tears
My head,
Full of fears, and
This conflict needs to end
So there can be peace in the land

The First Intifada was the time
I watched my brother *DIE*.
Pain,
Anger, and
Fear
Was all I felt
All the children want
Peace

Israelis
Palestinians

We both want the same thing.
This land we call Holy.
Can we live
In peace?
It's clear
That a child like me wants peace
For once can children be thought of?
All we want:
Peace

                  No more death

                                            No more crying

                  Only Peace

                  I believe

                  There is hope

                  That we can end this conflict

                  This pain that

                  Everyone suffers

                  With

                  Peace

                                            Love

Let's make it become part of our homelands. Is that too much?

FORGETTING
Sara Klinge

Forgetting
that it's not worth it
the silencing of children and all that was and is...
it's not worth it
why can't there be peace
As the darkness spread over the vast blanket of land
my mom told me to close my eyes...
and I enter a world of forgetting
I forget about my home in the Gaza strip
and I forget about
the intifada
and the bombing of the school buses
and I smile a real smile
something I had forgotten many years ago.
and I talk with my dad
as we once did so many years ago
before he was murdered,
before I forgave his attacker,
we sing and dance on what was
once our land...
our land....
the very thing this conflict is about
what we once called home has turned into a battlefield
and I remember
why can't there be love

or happy endings

does the world have to be so cold and unforgiving?

for now all we have are our dreams and we can go to them to forget

and forget we shall.

LIVE FOR THE FUTURE?
Shylyn Pinegar

I fail to understand why.

Why Palestinians and Israelis are still fighting.

Fighting over something that happened so long ago. Why must we live for the past?

Why can't we live for the future?

I hear the voice of the bomb.

Speaking to me.

Ever so angry.

I hear it again,

More angry than before. It sounds as if a ton of bricks are crashing down

on the cold world we live in.

CONFUSION

Samantha Vazquez

I am three
Mind-full of confusions
People running in fears
People shedding tears

I am Palestinian
I am Israeli

Mother lays in bed, nonstop conceives
When will her last tear be shed?
Will I grow up in this community full of fear?
Will I be in my brothers' army gear?

The Innocent try to arrange but
Many won't change

We want the Holy Land
They want the Holy Land

All- lost in translation
running around-the-block
like a ticking clock.

It's all a simple

Confusion

FINDING YOUR PEACE
Taylan Holland

There is peace.....
Where you would least expect it.
It is there
H
I
D
I
N
G
Waiting

for someone to find it...
it's not hidden far from the First Intifada…
around the corner from the Holocaust.

PEACE IS LIKE A GOLDEN BAR
Taylan Holland

Lives
that are gone
    c
    r
    y
    I
    n
    g
          there are tears.
But there is...
there is something good.
Through all the pain and through
all the tears.
THERE IS HOPE.

Somewhere in between these two kinds of people...
somewhere in between these actually not very different
people always out of reach

they both need to come....
come together and will one day have
    P
    E
    A
    C
    E

both sides wishing for
something
better...
someday is now. Now there is peace.

UNTITLED
Veronica Chavez

Day to day, souls pass on
    from set off, to the rise of the sun
    Palestinians from our would in risk of harm
unable to give them protection under our arm.

    Lives lost in plain sight of day
  why, oh, why is cruel life in such way?

        Fly away baby bird,
  fly away
where arrogance & war won't reach you
    fly away baby bird, fly away
where death & sorrow can't eat you

When two people are promised land
    who's at fault?
who's the owner of these beautiful beaches of sand

Fly away baby bird, fly away
where arrogance & war won't reach you
    fly away baby bird, fly away
where death & sorrow can't eat you

      forgive
        & relive

It's an Israeli Palestinian tear,
you are all in fear

I know you're sad you lost to whom you belong
strong,
do it for your family
this is reality

PEACE MY LAND AND YOURS
Shania Burton

Every day is a new life,
For I have survived my other one.
I don't want to die,
I want to live.

For life is something I want to treasure every day;
To live life to the fullest each day.
I don't want to die,
I have so much to live for.
I want to make peace.
I want to change the way things are.

I don't want to see
families losing loved ones.
I don't just want to end their sorrow,
I want to end this conflict,
Once and for all.

www.ingramcontent.com/pod-product-compliance
Lightning Source LLC
Chambersburg PA
CBHW032211040426
42449CB00005B/541